40
OBJECT SERMONS
FOR CHILDREN

40
OBJECT SERMONS FOR CHILDREN

JOE E. TRULL

BAKER BOOK HOUSE
Grand Rapids, Michigan 49516

Scripture quotations from *The Living Bible (TLB)* are
used by permission.

Copyright 1975 by
BAKER BOOK HOUSE COMPANY

ISBN: 0-8010-8831-3

First printing, November 1975
Second printing, November 1976
Third printing, August 1978
Fourth printing, August 1980
Fifth printing, August 1982
Sixth printing, March 1984
Seventh printing, November 1985
Eighth printing, July 1987
Ninth printing, November 1988

PHOTOLITHOPRINTED BY CUSHING - MALLOY, INC.
ANN ARBOR, MICHIGAN, UNITED STATES OF AMERICA

to

the children of Crestview Baptist Church
who first heard these sermons

CONTENTS

LEARNING ABOUT OTHERS

SPECIAL OCCASIONS

INTRODUCTION

What do you do with children? During worship, I mean. Let them sleep in mother's lap? Or scratch an abstract drawing onto the bulletin? As they get restless, a bribe of candy or gum will quiet them for a little while. Sometimes a mother's threatening pinch is used to ensure "reverence." Surely there is something better for children during the church service.

As both preacher and parent, I have felt plagued by this problem. The idea of a separate church service for youngsters was an alternative, but I decided that this created more problems than it solved. For many years I had planned to add a children's sermon to the morning service. Not just to eliminate the normal restlessness of children, but primarily to involve them in the act of worship. To help them feel part of the service and for them to gain some relevant truth for their life.

With the deep conviction that worship should be a family experience, I incorporated a three-minute sermon each Sunday morning for children four through eleven years old. Little did I realize what an impact this addition would have on both the children and the church. Jesus' words, "Suffer little children, and forbid them not to come unto me" (Matt. 19:14), took on new significance.

This special time for the children has become one of the most significant and responsive moments in our worship. I now wonder why I didn't begin sooner.

BASIC PRINCIPLES

A successful children's sermon doesn't just happen. Experience has shown that there are basic rules to follow. To overlook any of these principles is to run the risk of "bombing out." On the other hand, proper recognition of these rules of thumb will ensure a fruitful worship experience.

First, base each sermon on a simple and understandable purpose. A good way to begin is to write the main purpose in one sentence. A recent children's sermon, using a telephone as a prop, had the simple purpose—"to teach that prayer is talking to God." As you are writing this purpose, remember that you will be addressing preschoolers. They live in a different world. Adult concerns about bank accounts and buildings are foreign to their thinking.

A second principle: keep it brief. Children have a very short attention span. An ideal time limit is about three minutes. To say what needs to be said, and to say it well in capsule form, requires thorough preparation.

Talk to the children on their eye level. At the appointed time when our children come forward to sit on the floor around me, I like to squat down. Some pastors sit on the steps. However you do it, eye-to-eye contact is imperative. Be sure to look around the circle and speak directly to each child.

A wise pastor also learns how to talk and think on the same level with the children. Writing out the sermon beforehand allows the preacher to double check his vocabulary and syntax. If you have a willing child of your own with whom you can preview the sermon, vague words, complex sentences, and abstract thoughts can be uncovered and eliminated.

Above all, use familiar objects to illustrate your sermon. The right prop will do wonders. A few times I have tried to get by without a visual aid and have barely survived. What a difference it makes! For an Easter message, I used a cocoon to explain how a caterpillar becomes a butterfly. On another occasion red cellophane paper helped get across the point that God sees people, not skin color. "Pencils and People" was the title of a sermon stressing differences (size, shape, color) and similarities amongst people. The pencil underscored that man, like a pencil, has a purpose, makes mistakes, and sometimes gets broken. Put your imagination to work and you will find ways of using play dough, soap bubbles, maps, and other familiar props.

A principle that contains risks is allowing the children to participate. One easy approach is to let them handle and share the object, which is fine unless someone gets selfish. (Have you ever tried to referee a tug of war between children?) Asking questions can also be helpful. However, answers are unpredictable. When a group of children was asked if anyone knew what the offering plate was, one boy quickly replied, "It's an ash tray!" And once children start responding, it's often hard to get them to stop. A person should carefully plan any involvement of the children, then be ready for anything.

One final principle. Always close with a brief prayer that restates the central truth. This will reinforce this truth as well as teach the children conversational prayer.

These principles are by no means exhaustive or inviolable. However, most major problems which arise while delivering a children's sermon stem from the violation of one or more of these principles.

One of the interesting things I learned while giving children's sermons was how closely adults are listening. Some grownups have difficulty grasping abstract truth and thus relate more easily to the children's message. Don't be surprised to hear an adult say he gets more from the children's version. For many it becomes the favorite time of the service. The fact that adults are listening also affords an opportunity to slip in a sentence that speaks to them. In a children's sermon dealing with racial prejudice, I said, "Like God, most of you children are color blind. But soon some of us older folks will try to change you. We will teach you to see the color of people." The adults caught the point.

PROBLEMS

Certain problems are also involved in delivering a children's sermon. Perhaps the greatest preliminary problem is being unable to capture the children's attention. Nothing is quite as disconcerting as to realize that children are not listening. Adults may pretend to be interested in a dull sermon, but children are brutally honest. If you struggle through a sermon that fails to captivate children, evaluate the session using the principles listed above. Usually some basic rule has been overlooked.

Another danger is the hyperactive child. One bad apple can spoil the entire group. How do you handle a busybody who constantly fidgets, talks to others, pinches his neighbor, or distracts the group? First, don't let it upset you. Everyone expects children to be children. Next, try to involve the active child. Sometimes, a straightforward "Let's be still now so the other children can listen" is necessary. In extreme cases, a conference with parent and child may be needed to help the youngster grow in social awareness.

A related problem is uncontrolled conversation. A child does not have to be hyperactive to want to share experiences that distract from the theme of the sermon. The wise pastor will learn how to break in and move the conversation back to the lesson without seeming to dominate and manipulate. I am often amazed how a seemingly unrelated comment by a child can become rich insight for the sermon. In a children's sermon explaining the deceptiveness of sin, a fishhook was used. One boy broke in to tell about getting a hook in his finger. His experience drove home the truth of the sermon.

Perhaps the greatest problem is laziness—of the preacher, I mean. Most pastors could give a children's sermon impromptu, and get by. How easy, also, to simply parrot a canned message from one of the many resource books. Most books of children's sermons seem to have been written for preachers rather than children. So, do your own work. Spend the time necessary to make the message clear, concise, attractive, and personal.

Children are like play dough—easily molded and shaped. It is important to help them discover God early in life. I am convinced that an effective children's sermon each Sunday can be a powerful influence in the developing spiritual awareness of children in the church.

1

GOD'S HEARTBEAT

Object: *A stethoscope.*
Purpose: *To create an awareness of the reality*
            of God.

Look at what I have! A stethoscope (*display*). If
you have visited a doctor, you have probably seen
one of these. When we are sick, our doctor needs
to listen to our heartbeat. This instrument is what
he uses to hear the heart inside of us. Sometimes
doctors wear them like this (*demonstrate*).

If you put these two ends in your ears
(*demonstrate*), and if you place this flat part on a
person's chest, you will hear something. Ker-
thump, ker-thump, ker-thump. It's the beat of the
heart as it pumps blood throughout the body.

Let's have one of you listen to your own heartbeat. (*Select a child and place the tubes of the
stethoscope in his ears and the endpiece on his
chest.*) Did you hear your heartbeat? (*Pause for
response.*)

Have you ever heard God's heartbeat? Sometimes our hearts are touched in church. We sense God's presence, we know He is very near, and we feel very good. Why? Is it the lovely music of the organ? Or is it the beautiful hymns we sing? Or could it be the preaching of the Bible that we hear? Or maybe just the quietness of prayer as we talk to God?

But I wonder. Somehow I think it is more than all these things. The heartbeat of God is knowing that He is alive and at work in the world. When we worship in God's house and sense God's presence, we hear the heartbeat of God.

Listen! Do you hear it? God's heartbeat. God is alive and working right now in our hearts.

Prayer: Father, we are so glad that You are real; that You are as near as our heartbeat; that You are alive and at work in the world. Thank You for being real to me. Amen.

2

GOD AND THE WIND

Object: *Bits of confetti paper.*
Purpose: *To show the reality of God at work in the world.*

I was awakened last night by the wind blowing. The lightning was flashing and the thunder was crashing. When the wind blows, you can hear it whistling through the trees.

How many of you have seen the wind? (*Pause.*) You know, I don't think you really have seen the wind. I'll tell you why. Put your hand in front of your face. Now blow on your hand. Did you see anything? What did you see? Do it again! (*Pause.*) Did you see anything? Or did you *feel* something? You felt something, didn't you?

You really don't see the wind. What we see is what the wind does. Many times when you are outside and there are leaves hanging on the tree, the wind comes along and blows the leaves like this (*blow the confetti over the children*). The leaves all flutter down and you think you are seeing the wind. But you are not really seeing the wind, you are seeing the leaves and what the wind does to the leaves. So we really don't see the wind, although it is there. We just see what the wind does.

One day Jesus was talking about God, and He said that God is like the wind. Jesus meant that you can't see God, but He is real. The wind is real, but you can't see it. And God is real, even though you can't see Him.

But like the wind, you can see what God does. Just as you see leaves blown by the wind and trees bending in the wind, you can look at people and see the way God moves people. God is at work in the world. We can't see God, but we can see the results of God working in the lives of people. And that's one of the ways we know God is real.

The next time you hear the wind, the next time you see the trees blowing, the next time you see leaves floating in the air—think of God. And remember that God is like the wind. You don't see Him, but He is real. You do see what He does in the world. God is at work in the world, and you can see what He is doing, if you look around. Let's thank God for that.

Prayer: Dear God, thank You for the wind that cools my face, that brings the rain, and that reminds me that You are at work in the world though I can't see You. Amen.

3

A LOST COIN

Object: *An old (preferably ancient) coin.*
Purpose: *To teach the importance of every person
in God's sight.*

Recently I visited the country of Lebanon. It's a
very old country with places called *ruins*, where
people used to live many, many years ago. One
place we visited is named Baalbek. It was an old
Roman town. We saw the remains of many tem-
ples, buildings, and statues thousands of years old.

As we were leaving, a young boy ran up and
offered to sell me some old coins. I did buy this one
silver coin from him (*display*). This coin is a de-
narius, a piece of money Jesus used. It is probably
about 2000 years old. Evidently someone lost this
coin. It might have been a farmer, plowing in his
field, and the coin fell out of his pocket onto the
ground. Years later, someone saw something shin-
ing in the soil and found this old silver coin.

The Bible tells a story about a woman in Jesus'
day who lost a coin just like this one. She searched

and searched, looking in every corner of her house, until she found it. Then she was very, very happy.

"God is like that," said Jesus. You and I get lost—away from God. We are like a lost coin. But God loves us so much He cannot be happy until we are found. He searches and searches for us until one day we are found, and we belong to God again. That makes Him very happy.

If you ever feel lost, like a coin which has slipped out of God's hands, remember this—God knows you and He will help you find your way back to Him. He doesn't want any of us to be lost. That is why the Bible says that God searches for us just like the lady who lost the silver coin. And when He finds us and we find Him, God is very happy.

Prayer: Father, I am so glad that You miss us when we are lost; that You search for us until we are found. Thank You, God, for caring so much about every one of us. Amen.

4

A BROKEN WATCH

Object: *A watch that is broken or stopped.*
Purpose: *To teach God's power to create and transform.*

Here on my wrist I wear a watch. Look at it (*remove and display*). It's very pretty, isn't it? Shiny and bright, you can easily read the time on it's face.

Yet there's one thing wrong. Listen—it isn't ticking! (*Pause.*) Look—the watch says ten minutes after eight (*display again*). That's the wrong time!

Yes, you guessed it, the watch is broken or stopped. It is not running. What good is a watch that has stopped? Well, it might make a pretty bracelet for your arm. You could wear it to look pretty. But it surely isn't doing what it is supposed to do.

A watch is for telling time. If it doesn't tell you the time of day, then it isn't doing what it was made to do.

Did you know that many people are like this watch? They aren't doing what they were made to do.

They seem to be alive. But they really aren't. They don't have the life that God gives to all who believe in Him. They are broken, just like this watch.

But look. If I put a new battery in this watch (*demonstrate*), guess what happens? It begins to run again, to do what it was made to do.

Now that is exactly what God does to us when we trust in Jesus. He puts a new battery in us. God gives us new power. Then we really start to live the way God intended us to live.

God is like a watchmaker. He put us together. He knows what makes us tick. And He can give us a new battery—new power—that starts us running again.

God is in the business of taking broken things like you and me, fixing us up, and getting us started again.

Prayer: Dear God, sometimes the beautiful life You made in us gets broken by sin. Forgive us, fix us up, and help us to start running again—to do what we are supposed to do. Amen.

5

THE BOY AND THE ANT

Object: *An ant in a jar.*
Purpose: *To teach that God became a man in Jesus to reveal Himself to us.*

One time a little boy was walking with his father in the park. The young boy enjoyed running by the river, sitting under the trees, and skipping across the grassy hills.

Suddenly the boy looked down. He had stepped on an ant hill full of ants like this one (*display*). His foot had mashed the little pile of sand which was their home. He had also crushed several ants.

Being a little boy, and never having been stung by an ant, the youngster was sad. He said to his father, "Daddy, I've killed some ants. I didn't mean to. I didn't see the ants until after I had stepped on them. I wish I could become an ant and tell them I'm sorry."

Now you can't talk to ants. They just don't

understand human talk. So the boy felt there was no way he could tell them he was sorry except by becoming an ant.

God did something like that for us. He looked down on the world, and we were like little ants. God saw us running here and there, not even knowing He was looking at us or cared about us. So God said, "I know what I'll do. I'll become one of them—a man. Then I can tell them I love them and show them how much I care about them."

That's what God did for us when Jesus was born. God became a man to show us His love. God lived in our world in the life of Jesus. He talked to us in words we could understand.

Now we know what God is like. Jesus showed us. Jesus is God who became a man.

Prayer: Dear Father, thank You for becoming a person like me. Thank You for Jesus who showed me all about God. Amen.

6

THE CARPENTER

Object: *A wooden letter opener and two pieces of wood.*

Purpose: *To teach that Jesus died on a cross for our sins.*

In Israel a few months ago I saw a very interesting sight. A carpenter at work carving objects out of olive wood. Here is something he made—a hand-carved letter opener (*display*).

This carpenter had a special desk in a large building where he worked. Wood shavings were everywhere—on the floor, on his table, and even in his hair. Holding his knife in one hand, he slowly changed a branch from an olive tree into this beautiful letter opener.

Did you know that Jesus was a carpenter? He too worked with wood. As he grew up in Nazareth, he helped his father, Joseph, in the carpenter shop.

Being the son of a carpenter, Jesus soon learned how to make tables, chairs, and other wooden objects.

Jesus also died on a wooden object—a cross. The cross was two pieces of wood that looked like this (*make a cross with two pieces of wood*). Roman soldiers used wooden crosses to put people to death. Jesus, who worked with wood as a boy, also died on wood as a man.

Jesus' death was special though. God was showing us that He loved us and wanted to help us. Jesus died on a cross for our sins. That is why the Bible says, "For God loved the world so much that He gave His only Son so that anyone who believes in Him shall not perish but have eternal life" (John 3:16, TLB).

Prayer: Thank You, God, for sending Jesus to die on the cross for my sin. Amen.

7

A PICTURE OF GOD

Object: *Family pictures and a picture of Jesus.*
Purpose: *To teach that Jesus Christ is God.*

Here are some pictures from my desk (*display*). These are pictures of my family. Here is my wife. This is my oldest daughter, this is my son, and this is my youngest child. We like pictures because they remind us of persons, usually persons we love very much.

Have you ever seen a picture of Jesus? Well, no one knows for sure what Jesus looked like. There are many pictures and paintings that show what men think He looked like. Here is a portrait of Jesus Christ painted by a famous artist named Rembrandt (*display*). We are not certain how Jesus actually looked, but He probably looked like most of the men of His day, something like this picture.

Have you ever seen a picture of God? No man has ever seen God. That's probably why we don't have pictures of God. Yet, do you know what the Bible says? It says that Jesus is a portrait, a picture of God. If you want to know what God is really like, just look at Jesus. He is the exact picture of God.

You see, Jesus is God living in a human body. As we see Jesus, God's Son, we really see God. For you see, Jesus is God living in a human body. That is why Jesus once said, "Anyone who has seen me has seen the Father" (John 14:9, TLB).

Prayer: Father, thank You for sending Your Son Jesus into the world so that we could know what You are like. Amen.

8

GOD'S BINOCULARS

Object: *A pair of binoculars.*
Purpose: *To teach that Jesus provides us a close-up view of God.*

This spring we hung a birdfeeder in the large oak tree in our back yard. Soon all kinds of birds were chirping and scratching as they ate the seeds. We saw beautiful red cardinals, brown doves, grey sparrows, velvet-breasted wrens, and even one bunting colored green, blue, and red.

Every time one of our family saw a new bird, he would cry, "Quick, get the binoculars! There is a different bird at the feeder."

Have you ever used binoculars? Here is a pair (*display*). Binoculars are special glasses through which you look. Sights that are very far away are made to look close. When I put these binoculars up to my eyes like this (*demonstrate*), the birds that were very small and hard to see suddenly look very close and easy to see.

Before Jesus was born, people felt that God was very far away. They wondered what God was like. Was He kind or was He cruel? Was He powerful or weak? Was God good or bad? No one knew for sure.

Then Jesus came. Jesus was God's binoculars. How? By looking at Jesus you could see God. God who seemed far away was now close. To see Jesus was to see God up close. Jesus was God's binoculars.

Maybe you have thought of God as being far, far away. He isn't, really. He is just as close as Jesus. Look at Jesus, and you will see God.

Prayer: Dear God, I'm glad to know that You are my heavenly Father and You love me. I'm glad that Jesus lived to show me how good You really are. Thank You, God, for Jesus. Amen.

9

FLOWERS

Object: *A flower for each child.*
Purpose: *To teach God's daily care.*

Look what I have for you this morning. Flowers! Here is one for each of you (*give each child a flower*). As you take your flower, I want you to do a few things for me.

First, look at your flower very closely. (*Pause.*) Flowers attract us because they are pretty. Notice your flower. See the colors—pink and yellow and green. Look at the petals. Each one is shaped a very special way.

Now let's do something else. Let's smell our flowers. Ummm. Isn't that a pleasant fragrance? Another reason we like flowers is because they smell so good.

Now do one other thing. Touch your flower. Feel its softness? Flowers are nice to touch. When God made flowers, He made a beautiful creation.

Jesus talked about flowers once. The people were worried about food to eat and clothes to wear. In Matthew 6:28-30, Jesus told them not to worry. Jesus reminded them to look at the flowers in the fields to see how beautiful they are. If God takes care of the flowers, He will also take care of people.

Flowers remind us of God's care. Just as He made them, He made us. And just as He clothes them in colors more beautiful than a king's robe, so He will take care of our needs too.

"So, don't worry," said Jesus. The God who made the flowers, made you. And He loves you even more than He loves the flowers He made. You can be certain He will take care of you.

Prayer: Thank You, God, for beautiful flowers. And thank You for taking care of me every day. Amen.

10

I FORGOT

Object: *A piece of string.*
Purpose: *To teach God's constant care and His willingness to forgive and forget our sins.*

Last Sunday morning as I was hurrying to church, I forgot something. It was a pair of binoculars. I needed them for the children's sermon. I was very upset that I had forgotten the binoculars because I didn't have time to return home to get them. So I had to find something else to use that day.

Have you ever forgotten something? Sometimes people use a string to help them remember something they don't want to forget (*display*). Tying a string around your finger is a reminder.

Suppose your mother said, "Tomorrow I want you to bathe your dog." How can you remember to do that? One way is to take a string, tie it on your finger (*demonstrate*), and then, when you wake the next day and see the string, you will say, "This string reminds me that today I'm supposed to give my dog a bath.''

We forget sometimes, don't we? The Bible says, however, that God never forgets. He never forgets to love us, to watch over us, to care for us, and to protect us. Even when we are sleeping, God is there. He remembers all about us.

The Bible says there is only one thing God forgets—*our sin*. When we do wrong, there is a string tied around God's finger (*tie string on your finger*). But when we say to God, "I'm sorry, forgive me, Lord, of my sins," that instant God unties the string and throws it away (*untie string and throw aside*). He remembers our sin no more.

Isn't that wonderful? God knows all about us. He *remembers* to care for us. And he *forgets* our sins. Let's thank Him for that.

Prayer: Dear God, thank You for remembering us every day. And thank You for forgiving and forgetting our sins. Amen.

11

LOOK FOR THE HOOK

Object: *A small fish hook.*
Purpose: *To teach the attractiveness and danger of sin.*

A few weeks ago I was fishing for trout in a beautiful lake in northern New Mexico. This is what I used—it's a very small fish hook (*display*). It's small because trout have small mouths.

To catch a trout, you take a salmon egg—a round, bright-red egg about the size of a green pea and place it on the hook. Then you drop the baited hook to the bottom of the lake, and wait.

A trout will come along (*dramatize*). He'll see the delicious looking salmon egg, swoop down, and with one gulp, take it into his mouth. At that moment you will feel a tug on your fishing line. If you jerk on the line, the hook will set into the fish's mouth. Then you reel in the fish that you have caught.

There are many things in the world that look beautiful, but they have a hook. The Bible calls these things *sin*. Sin is often attractive. It looks delicious. But if you look very closely, you'll see the hook. The hook is that sin always hurts people. It may hurt you. It may hurt someone else. Sin always has a hook in it. And Satan loves to throw out his bait, hook us, and reel us in and away from God.

So when you are tempted to do wrong, always remember to look for the hook. Sin, like the salmon egg, looks delicious. But hidden beneath the surface is a hook. If you swallow the bait, you'll get hooked every time. Don't be fooled by sin. It has a hook. And it hurts. Always look for the hook.

Prayer: Dear God, when we are tempted to do wrong, help us to see the hook. Don't let sin hurt us and take us away from You. Amen.

12

PENCILS AND PEOPLE

Object: *Five pencils (red, yellow, black, brown, and white) of various sizes.*

Purpose: *To show that we all need forgiveness.*

Today I have in my hand five pencils. We use pencils every day, don't we? To draw pictures, to write numbers, and to spell words.

Did you know that pencils are like people? They really are. Look at these five pencils I am holding in my hand. How do they remind you of people? (*Pause long enough to give the children the opportunity to discover some answers.*)

Yes, people, like pencils, come in all sizes. Some are short, like this pencil (*display*), and some are tall, like this one (*display*). Some are slender and some are large (*display*).

Also, people are different in color. Look at your hair—some of you are red-headed, some are blond, some have brown hair, and some have black hair. Look at your skin. Mine is white and brown. Others have black skin, or reddish skin, or yellowish skin. So people, like pencils, come in different colors.

But there's one very important way pencils are like people. Look here. What is this on the top of every pencil? That's right, it's an eraser. And why do pencils have erasers? (*Pause.*) That's right, so that mistakes can be erased.

People make mistakes. Every day. The Bible calls our mistakes *sin*. Sin is disobeying God. Sin is doing wrong. Sin is making a mistake.

What can you do when you make a mistake? Well, the Bible says that God wants to erase your mistakes. David, the shepherd boy who became king, once prayed to God and asked God to erase his mistakes in Psalm 51:1, that is, to forgive his sin.

God has promised in the Bible that the very moment we ask Him, He will forgive our sins. In I John 1:9 God tells us that if we tell Him our sins, our mistakes, He will forgive us and cleanse or erase all our wrongdoings. Let's pray to God right now and ask Him to erase our sins.

Prayer: Dear God, every time we see an eraser on a pencil we remember that we make mistakes. We also know You love us and want to erase our mistakes. So, God, please forgive us our sins and erase our mistakes that we may be clean. Amen.

13

AIR

Object: *An empty jar or bottle.*
Purpose: *To teach that salvation is necessary and free.*

I have something very important in this jar (*display*). Do you know what it is? Let me give you some clues. It has no color, no taste, and is very light. You can't live without it. Yet, it's free. Does anyone want to guess? (*Pause.*) Yes, it's the air we breathe. Air is a free gift of God. All the air we want to breathe every day. It's all around us.

Let's do something. Let's pretend we don't want God's free gift of air. Let's just not use it. Now let's all hold our breath, and not breathe, okay? (*Pause as you lead the children in holding their breath.*)

Well, maybe I should change my mind and take this gift of air after all. Even though I can't buy it, it's very important. I would die without it.

Did you know that God has another gift that's free? And this gift is so much more valuable than air. This gift is His Son, the Lord Jesus Christ, whom God gave to the world long ago. The Bible says, "For God so loved the world, that He gave His only begotten Son" (John 3:16).

But suppose I don't want that free gift. Suppose I decide to say no to Jesus Christ. What happens? It's like holding my breath. If I refuse God's gift of Jesus, I will die. Jesus Christ is necessary for life, just as air is necessary for living.

You and I cannot live without air. And we cannot have real life without Jesus either. He is life. To have Jesus is like breathing fresh, clean air. It's life at its best—*eternal life* the Bible calls it. Listen to these words from the Bible: "the gift of God is eternal life through Jesus Christ our Lord" (Rom. 6:23).

Prayer: Thank You, Father, for Your Son, Jesus Christ, and for the life He freely gives to all who believe in Him. Amen.

14

FAITH AND A CHAIR

Object: *A chair.*
Purpose: *To teach the nature of faith in Christ.*

After a long, tiring day, I like to go home and sit down in a chair like this to rest (*display but do not sit down*). Chairs are for resting. But how do you know if you can trust a chair to hold you up? How can I be sure that this chair will not fall apart when I sit down in it?

Well, first, I can look it over. It seems to be a good chair. It looks sturdy. I think it will hold me up. But I don't know for sure, do I?

Another way is to find out who made the chair. If it has been put together by a good company, I can trust it to hold me up. This chair was made by a good company (*display brand*). Since they make good chairs, I can trust this one to hold me up. Yet, I still am not positive this chair is sturdy.

When do I *really* know I can trust this chair? (*Pause.*) That's right, when I sit down in it (*sit down*). That's when I really *believe* in the chair. When I trust myself to it. When I have faith in it.

Having faith in Jesus is like trusting in this chair.

I might look Jesus Christ over and say, "I think He is worth trusting. He looks good and sturdy." But I don't know for sure, do I? Not just by looking. That's not faith.

I may even say, "I believe in the Maker—God. He sent Jesus into the world. God can be trusted. He is a good Maker." Just believing that the One who made Jesus is reliable is not enough either. Faith is more than saying God is reliable.

What then is real faith? What is complete trust in Jesus? It's when I put myself into His hands. Just as trusting in this chair requires me to sit in it (*demonstrate*), so trusting in Jesus requires putting my life in His hands. To believe in Jesus is like sitting in a chair; it is trusting Jesus completely with my life. Have you ever done that? I hope you will.

Prayer: Dear Lord, help each of these boys and girls to trust in Jesus completely, putting his or her life in His hands. Amen.

15

MOSQUITOES AND SIN

Object: *A can of insect repellent.*
Purpose: *To teach the power of the Bible to protect against sin (Ps. 119:11).*

Have you ever been bitten by a mosquito? A few weeks ago I was mowing the lawn in our back yard. Suddenly, several mosquitoes were on my skin and began biting me. They were on my arm, my neck, and my legs. There were so many of them, I ran for the house. Large welts rose on my skin where these tiny black insects had enjoyed a meal of my flesh and blood.

The lawn still had to be mowed. How could I do it? There was one way to go outside without getting bitten—*insect repellent!*

I went to the cabinet and took this can (*display*). It contains a liquid that mosquitoes don't like. Putting it on your body keeps them away. So, I rubbed this liquid all over my neck, my arms, and my legs. Then I went outside and mowed the lawn without any bother from the mosquitoes.

There is something worse than mosquito bites. And that is *sin*. Sin is disobeying God. Sin takes us away from God. But there is a way you and I can be protected from sin. A verse in the Book of Psalms reads, "Thy word have I hid in mine heart, that I might not sin against thee" (Ps. 119:11).

The Bible is God's sin repellent. The more we read it, study it, hear it taught, and live it; the more we keep sin out of our life. Just as this insect repellent keeps mosquitoes away, so the Bible keeps sin away.

The insect repellent I put on last week won't keep mosquitoes away today. It has to be applied again and again. The Bible also has to be put in our heart week by week. It can't be left on a shelf and not used.

So, read the Bible. Hear it. Study it. Learn from it. Live as it says. In that way you will protect your life from sin and you will make God very happy. "Thy word have I hid in mine heart, that I might not sin against thee." Can you say that with me? (*Repeat words slowly, helping children say the verse.*)

Prayer: Dear Lord, thank You for Your Word, the Bible. Help each boy and girl to hide the words of the Bible in their heart, so they will be protected from sin. Amen.

16

BOOKS AND COVERS

Object: *A book.*
Purpose: *To teach that a person's inner life is more important than external appearance.*

I like books. Do you? Here is one from our church library (*display*). The name of this book is *My Good Shepherd*. It's a Bible storybook.

Books are a lot like people. They have a cover (*display*). So do we. All books look a certain way on the outside. But they also have an inside (*flip pages*). Sometimes the inside is much different from the outside. There is a saying: "You can't judge a book by its cover." That means, you can't tell what is inside just by looking at the cover.

People are like that too. Sometimes you may see a person and say to yourself, "That boy sure looks mean!" But when you get to know him, you find he is very nice and kind. Or you may see a girl and say, "Isn't she beautiful?" Then you get to know her and you find out that she is ugly inside. You can't judge people by their covers.

The Bible says that too. Listen to what God once spoke to Samuel: ". . . for man looketh on the outward appearance, but the Lord looketh on the heart" (I Sam. 16:7). That means the most important part of a person, like a book, is not the outside. It's what's inside that counts. God looks into our hearts. That's where we decide how to live.

God says we should not judge people by their cover. Whether they are white, black, red, or brown doesn't really matter. Tall or short, thin or fat, nice-looking or unattractive—that really doesn't matter either. It's what's inside that counts. God looks on our hearts. How we really feel and think and live on the inside is the most important thing about us.

So, when you see a book, remember this truth. For both people and books, it's what's inside that counts.

Prayer: Lord, give us eyes to see people like You see them. Help us know that the outside doesn't matter, it's what's inside a person that really counts. Amen.

17

GOD AND PLAY DOUGH

Object: *A can of play dough or silly putty.*
Purpose: *To show how God can mold our lives.*

Do you see what I have this morning? (*Display.*)
A can of play dough. How many of you have
played with play dough? What can you do with
play dough? (*Give time for responses to both
questions.*)

Yes, play dough is a pretty clay that's very soft.
You can take it like this (*work in hand*) and use it to
make all sorts of things—pancakes (*press flat and
display*), snakes (*roll thin and display*), doughnuts
(*connect the ends of the snake and display*), and all
kinds of shapes.

Did you know the Bible says that we are like
play dough in God's hands? Listen to these words
from Isaiah 64:8:

> . . . Lord, thou art our Father;
> we are the clay, and thou our potter;
> and we all are the work of thy hand.

This means our lives are like play dough. God
wants to take our lives and to shape them into
something very beautiful (*work the play dough into*

a figure and display). But if we mold our own lives, they get all twisted out of shape (*twist play dough into a grotesque figure and display*).

What happens if you leave the play dough outside the container and it gets old? (*Pause.*) That's right, it becomes hard. So hard you can't mold it.

That is why God wants to mold us when we are young. If we wait too long to let God take us in His hands, we get hard—too hard for God to shape us the way He wants us to be. That is why we should let God have our lives while we are young. That's the very best time for God to mold us.

For our prayer, I want to read the words of a song we sing in church. This song asks God to take us, like clay, and mold us. Listen to the words as we bow our heads and pray.

Prayer: Have Thine own way, Lord!
Have Thine own way!
Thou art the Potter,
I am the clay.
Mold me and make me
after Thy will,
While I am waiting,
yielded and still. Amen.

18

LOST

Object: *A road map.*
Purpose: *To teach God's guidance of our lives.*

Have you ever been lost? It's frightening not to know where you are, isn't it?

One time I was lost. I was driving my car in a very large city and I lost my way. I had a map, like this one (*unfold and display*). It showed the main streets in the city, but I couldn't figure out where I was. I was lost.

On and on I drove, hoping to find a familiar street. Finally I decided to stop and ask a lady who was walking along. "Sure," she said, "I know exactly where you are headed." She was eager to give me directions. Here is what she said: "Go south four blocks, turn right and go past a church, take a left at the second stop light, then at the second corner, turn right and you'll be there. You can't miss it."

But I did! Either I heard her wrong or I didn't follow her directions because I was still lost.

In desperation I stopped another person and told him my problem. "You're going in the wrong direction," he replied. "You'll never find the street you are looking for on your own. Here, let me go along with you. I'll show you the way." So, with my guide, away we went.

Living is very much like driving through a strange city. Day by day, as you try to find your way, you may become lost. Some people may give you wrong directions and say, "It doesn't matter how you live. Lie, cheat, steal, and forget about God! It doesn't matter."

Others may confuse you. "Do this." "Don't do that." "Live this way," they advise. However, rules for living are not enough. You need more than that.

What you and I need in life is someone who will guide us—someone who will show us the way. A person who doesn't just tell us how to live, but walks with us to help us find the right way.

The Bible says we do have such a guide. One who will lead us, guide us, and go with us. In fact, He said to people, "I am the way" (John 14:6). Do you know who said that? (*Pause*.) That's right. Jesus Christ is our daily guide.

Prayer: Thank You, Lord, for guiding our footsteps, for holding our hand, for walking by our side every day. Amen.

ACORNS AND OAK TREES

Object: *An acorn.*
Purpose: *To challenge children to grow up to be Christ-like.*

Do you have an oak tree in your yard? In our front yard we have two giant oak trees. They are so big that they're taller than our house! In the summer they shade our yard from the hot sun. Squirrels race up and down the trunk of the tree. Birds build nests high in its branches. There is even a beehive in one of the hollow limbs. When winter comes, the wind whistles through the branches, the limbs creak and sway, and the yellow leaves fall to the ground.

Do you know how a giant oak tree is born? Every oak tree started out as a little acorn (*display*). Did you know that? If you plant this acorn, it will grow to be a giant oak. This little acorn has locked up inside of it the power to be an oak tree. All the branches, leaves, and limbs of an oak tree are wrapped up right here inside this seed.

Did you know that it was the same way for you? When you first started growing, you were very small, smaller than an acorn. But wrapped inside the tiny cells that were you was all the potential of a person. Your eyes, your ears, your hands, your feet, and the color of your hair were all right there in the tiny seed that was you.

You may think right now you are just a little child, like this acorn. But in every one of you there is the possibility of becoming a big person. Not just big on the outside, but big on the inside—like Jesus was. Big in love, and truth, and goodness. The potential of being like Jesus, of living the way He lived. You might say there is a Jesus locked within all of us, ready to be unloosed if we let Him. Jesus wants to live in us and live through us and help us to become like Him.

Are you an acorn? Do you want to become an oak tree? You can!

Prayer: Dear Lord, help each of these little children know that they are like a little acorn now—very small. But soon they can become a giant person like Jesus. Help us all to grow up and become like Him. Amen.

20

GOD'S TELEPHONE NUMBER

Object: *A telephone.*
Purpose: *To teach that prayer is talking to God.*

Have you learned how to use the telephone? (*Display*.) Yes, you pick up the receiver, listen for the dial tone, then you dial the number of the person to whom you want to talk (*demonstrate*).

Isn't it amazing? By dialing certain numbers you can talk to someone far away—your grandmother in another state or your friend in another city!

Did you know that talking to God is like talking on a telephone? Yes, it really is. The Bible has a word for talking to God. The word is *prayer*. When we pray we are talking to God just like we talk to someone on the telephone. In fact, it's better.

When we talk to God in prayer, we don't have to be in a certain place. There are places where there are no telephones. But there is no place where you can't talk to God. You can pray anywhere.

Also, the line is never busy. Sometimes when we use the telephone, we hear a busy signal. That means someone is already talking on that phone. But you never get a buzz-buzz-buzz busy signal when you talk to God. He is always waiting to hear you pray.

Have you ever dialed a wrong number? I have. If your finger makes a mistake, you get the wrong person on the phone. This doesn't happen when you pray. When you talk to God, you always get the right Person.

One other thing. God always has something to say to you when you pray. Remember to listen. As you talk to God, He also has something He wants to say to you.

So, prayer is like talking on a telephone. Prayer is talking to God. It is like picking up the telephone in the morning (*pick up the receiver*) and saying: "Good morning, God. Thank you for today and the beautiful world all around me. I am so glad I can talk to you and tell you how I feel. Do you have something you want to say to me? I'm listening."

Tonight, before you go to bed, why not talk to God like that? He really wants to hear you talk to Him in prayer.

Prayer: Dear Father, teach each of us how to pray. Amen.

21

GOD'S FLASHLIGHT

Object: *A flashlight.*
Purpose: *To teach the importance of the Bible.*

Have you ever walked into a cave? Maybe you have visited Inner Space, or Wonder Cave, or Carlsbad Caverns. Once I was in a cavern, deep under the ground. Our guide led us along a rocky path. Suddenly, all the lights went out. It was dark—so dark you couldn't see anything. I stumbled over a rock and almost fell.

The guide said, "Don't anyone move! You could fall and hurt yourself. I have a flashlight." Then he turned on his flashlight (*display lighted flashlight*) and we could see again. With the aid of the flashlight we walked along the rocky ledge without tripping or falling. The light helped us get out of the cave safely.

Did you know that God has a flashlight? Psalm 119:105 says that the Bible is "a flashlight to light the path ahead of me, and keep me from stumbling" (TLB).

This means that the Bible helps us. When we might do something that would hurt us, the Bible says, "Watch out, there is a rock that will trip you." When we are headed in the wrong direction, the Bible says, "Look out, there is a deep pit over there that you can fall into and get hurt."

So the Bible is like a flashlight. Just as you carry a flashlight in your hand, you can carry the Bible in your heart. The more you read it, hear it, and live it, the happier you will be. The Bible will keep you from stumbling. It is God's flashlight. It will guide you through the darkest night.

Prayer: For the Bible, I thank You, God. It's words, like a flashlight, guide me every day. Help me carry the Bible in my heart. Amen.

22

HABITS

Object: *A toothbrush.*
Purpose: *To teach the importance of regular church attendance.*

Do you know what a habit is? A habit is something you do regularly that becomes natural for you. If you bite your fingernails every time you get nervous, that soon becomes a habit—a bad habit.

There are also good habits. See this toothbrush? (*Display.*) How many of you have a toothbrush? What do you use them for? When do you use them? (*Allow answers to each question.*)

That's right, we brush our teeth after every meal. Now, if you always brush your teeth after each meal, you soon make it a habit—the good habit of brushing your teeth. You do it regularly and it becomes natural to brush your teeth after eating.

If brushing your teeth after meals is a habit, you don't stop and ask, "Should I brush my teeth?" You just do it. It has become a good habit in your life.

There are other good habits too. Coming to church every Sunday is a good habit. If you have that habit in your life, you don't get up on Sunday morning and ask, "Shall we go to church?" You wake up on Sunday morning planning to go to church to worship God because you always attend church on Sunday. It has become a good habit in your life.

What happens if we don't brush our teeth? (*Allow someone to answer, "Cavities."*) Did you know that if we don't have the good habit of going to church each Sunday we also get cavities—spiritual cavities? Sin is a germ that creeps into our lives and causes black cavities in our heart. The more we worship God and study the Bible, the less chance we have of getting spiritual cavities. So, along with brushing your teeth, form the good habit of worshiping God every Sunday. It's one habit that is really good for your life.

Prayer: Dear Lord, help me to take as good care of my soul as I do of my teeth, by attending church every Sunday. Amen.

23

MIRROR, MIRROR

Object: *A hand mirror.*
Purpose: *To teach the joy of worship.*

"Mirror, mirror on the wall, who's the fairest of them all?" That's what the wicked witch asked as she looked in the mirror, in the fairy tale "Snow White."

We look in mirrors every day, don't we? And what do we see? (*Let children see themselves in the mirror.*) A freckle, long beautiful hair, a missing tooth, a dirty face, or a smile.

In a church in another country, the people have put a big mirror in their church. Do you know why? They want people who worship to see their own faces. The first step in worshiping God, they believe, is to be happy—to wear a smile. So they put a gigantic mirror on the wall at the front of their church. Everyone who worships sees himself and remembers to smile and be happy.

Maybe we need a big mirror here in our church. It might be good to see if we are really happy when we worship God.

We should be! There should be a big smile on our face when we sing, when we pray, when we listen, and when we serve God. Worshiping God is a joyful experience—like a party. A time to smile.

Look in this mirror. Are you happy? You should be, God loves you. That will give you a happy face any time.

Prayer: How happy we are today, God. We know You love us and care for us and that makes us glad. We love You too. Amen.

24

JESUS LOVES ME

Object: *A songbook.*
Purpose: *To teach that singing is a way to worship God.*

Do you hear the song the organist is playing? It is one which children like to sing. It's called "Jesus Loves Me." Have you ever sung that song? (*Pause.*)

The song is in this songbook (*display*). Do you know what a songbook is for? It is a book that helps us sing songs about God. That is one way we worship. Singing is a happy way to say to God, "Father, we love You." All of the songs we sing have words that tell us something about God.

Do you like to sing? (*Pause.*) I do. I like to worship God by singing songs that praise Him. Some songs thank Him, and some songs teach us how wonderful God is.

Would you like to sing a song right now? Let's sing "Jesus Loves Me." That's a good song to sing, because it tells us how much God loves every one of us (*lead the children in singing*).

> Jesus loves me!
> This I know,
> for the Bible
> Tells me so.
> Little ones to Him belong;
> they are weak but He is strong.
> Yes, Jesus loves me!
> Yes, Jesus loves me!
> Yes, Jesus loves me!
> The Bible tells me so.

Did you enjoy that? (*Pause.*) I did. Isn't it nice to sing about God? Let's thank God for beautiful music and the joy of singing.

Prayer: Dear God, how happy we are when we sing. Thank You for our voices. Thank You for the songs we sing. Thank You, God, for everything. Amen.

25

A SACK LUNCH

Object: *A lunch sack; five crackers; two sardines.*
Purpose: *The importance of giving God our goods.*

This morning I want to tell you a Bible story about a boy who lived when Jesus lived—long ago.

One morning he said, "Mother, may I go fishing with my friends?"

"All right," she said, "but let me fix you some lunch." (*Display lunch sack.*)

Since they were very poor, all his mother could put in his lunch sack was five pieces of dry bread. (*Display and insert crackers.*)

"I hope you catch some fish to eat with your lunch," she said.

Off he went with his friends toward their favorite fishing spot on the shore of the Sea of Galilee. After fishing for a few hours, the young lad had caught only two small fish (*display and put in sack.*) He was tired and ready to go home. Suddenly he saw something unusual—a crowd of people gathering on the hillside. As he went up, he couldn't see what was going on, so he got down on his hands and knees, crawling between the legs of the people, until at last he was at the front of the crowd. There he saw and heard a man named Jesus.

He stood there with his sack lunch in his hand, listening to Jesus speak. His parents had told him that Jesus was from God, a man who helped the sick to get well, the blind to see, and the lame to walk. How lucky he was to get to see Jesus himself.

It was lunch time and the people were hungry. One of Jesus' men standing alongside the boy said, "May I borrow your lunch?" The boy gave the man his bread and the two fish he had caught.

And do you know what? Jesus fed all those people—over 5000—with this little boy's lunch! Jesus made thousands of pieces of bread and fish out of one little boy's lunch.

Sometimes we think that what we have isn't much, just a few crackers and a couple of fish. But God is glad when we give Him what we have, for God always does so much with it. Whatever you give to God, He always does much more with it than we ever could. Let's pray that we may give God our best.

Prayer: Dear Father, take what I have—my hands, my feet, my voice, and my heart. Take my life and use it to help others. Amen.

26

A LETTER TO GOD

Object: *A box of offering envelopes and a sealed envelope.*

Purpose: *To teach that giving money to the church is one way of expressing love to God.*

Does anyone know what I have in my hand? (*Display*.) Inside this box are fifty-two envelopes (*remove one*). Can anyone tell me what these envelopes are used for? (*Pause*.) That's right. Each Sunday we put money in these envelopes and bring them to church.

What happens to our money? Well, all of the money is used to help people learn about Jesus. Some of the money helps to build our buildings. Our janitor is paid to keep the buildings clean week by week. Part of the money buys Bibles, Sunday school books, and lots of things we use to teach people about God. Another part of our money goes to other lands to help people learn about Jesus. The money we give helps many, many people both here in our city and all over the world.

There is another kind of envelope we use. This envelope (*display sealed envelope*) we find in our mailboxes. It is a letter. Have you ever sent a letter to someone? (*Pause.*)

Did you know that, in a way, our weekly offering envelope is a letter to God? When you and I give money in our envelopes, we are sending a special letter to God. Our offering envelope is a letter that tells God we love Him and want to help others know about Him.

So let's use our offering envelopes every Sunday. It's a very special way to send a letter to God and tell Him that we love Him.

Prayer: God, we love You very much and we are so glad we can give money to help others learn about Jesus like we have. Amen.

27

SEASHELLS

Object: *A seashell.*
Purpose: *To teach a Christian attitude toward death.*

Recently our family went to Galveston! Galveston is an island on the coast of Texas. Most people go there to see the ocean. There are so many fun things you can do. You can swim, make sand castles, watch the sea gulls, ride on a boat, or hunt for seashells.

Here is a seashell we found in Galveston (*display*.) You have probably held these to your ear to hear what sounds like the roar of the sea. Seashells come in all sizes and shapes. They are very pretty.

Do you know what a seashell really is? It is a house. A deserted house. A seashell is a house in which a snail once lived. After a time the snail leaves his house and the shell washes up on the beach for someone to find.

Did you know that our body is like this seashell? Our body is a house in which we live. When we die, we simply leave this house and go to God who gives us a new house in which to live. That is why the Bible says we don't have to be afraid to die.

Seashells are pretty. So are our bodies. But the new body God gives us after we die is much prettier and better than the body we have now. Dying is just leaving our seashell behind us and going to God to get a new body. That's one reason Jesus came. To tell us we do not have to fear death, that God will give us a new body in heaven when we die.

Prayer: Thank You, God, for taking care of us, for giving us bodies to live in now, and for taking us to heaven when we die to give us a new body even better than the one we have. Amen.

28

OUR TONGUE

Object: *Each person's tongue.*
Purpose: *To teach the importance of telling others about God.*

Today I want to talk to you about something every one of us has. You have it with you today. It's the strongest muscle in your body.

Is it your arm? (*Flex arm.*) No, it's not your arm muscle. Is it your leg? (*Kick leg.*) No, it's not your leg muscle. The strongest muscle in your body is your tongue (*open mouth and touch the tongue*). Did you know that? The tongue is the strongest muscle we have because we use it so much. I want everyone to open their mouth and touch their tongue. (*Pause.*)

How do we use our tongue?

Well, we use it to taste. Have you ever tasted sugar? It's sweet, isn't it? Have you ever tasted a lemon? It's bitter, isn't it? Tongues are for tasting.

It also helps us to swallow. While we are eating, our tongue helps move our food around in our mouth and send it on to our stomach.

But do you know the best way our tongues are used? For telling! Our tongues help us to talk. I'm using my tongue right now to talk to you and make words. Sounds like *tuh* and *lah* are made with the help of my tongue.

Jesus once told a man, "Go home to your friends and tell them what wonderful things God has done for you" (*Mark 5:19, TLB*). That is the very best way to use your tongue. To tell your friends what wonderful things God has done for you. Have you ever done that?

Prayer: Dear Father, thank You for our tongues. We are glad we can taste, and eat, and talk. Help us, Father, to use our tongues to tell others about You and Your Son, Jesus Christ. Amen.

29

GOING FISHING

Object: *A fishing rod and reel.*
Purpose: *To teach the importance of helping others learn about Jesus.*

Last week during a visit to the coast, I went fishing. Along with eleven others, early one morning I got on board a small fishing boat. Soon the motor began to chug-chug-chug as we tossed and swayed, heading out into the bay. The smell of the sea air was clean, and the touch of the sea breeze cool to our faces.

Soon we arrived at a fishing spot in the ocean. Everyone took his rod and reel and began to fish.

To catch fish you need a rod and reel like this one (*display*). Do you know how to use this? Here is what you do (*dramatize*). First, you bait the hook. We had small shrimp, which fish like to eat, to put on our hooks.

Then, you cast out your line. The weight on the end of the line carries the bait deep into the water.

Finally, you wait for a bite. This is the hardest part. Soon I felt a tug on the line. That meant a fish was eating the bait. I jerked on the line to catch the fish, then I reeled in a beautiful sand trout.

Did you know that Jesus was a fisherman? Jesus once told His helpers, "Follow me, and I will make you fishers of men" (*Matt. 4:19*). Did you know that's what Jesus wants us to be—fishers of men?

What do you think Jesus meant by those words? No, He doesn't want us to take a rod and reel and bait to hook people. What He really wants is for you and me to *catch* people. To help people find God by going after them just like we go after fish when we are fishing.

I was excited last week because I caught twenty-seven fish. We also get excited when we catch someone for God. You and I can be God's fishermen. How? By helping others find out about God.

We catch men by bringing them to God's house to learn about Jesus. We fish for men when we tell people that God loves them. By bringing people to God, we are fishers of men.

Prayer: Dear God, help us this week to be a fisher of men by bringing someone to Jesus. Amen.

30

EMPTY SHOES

Object: *A pair of shoes.*
Purpose: *To teach the value of serving Christ, especially as a missionary.*

Many years ago in England there lived a man named William Carey, who was a cobbler. Do you know what a cobbler is? He is a man who makes shoes (*display*).

Well, day after day, William Carey sat at his bench, nailing heels on shoes, sewing the leather together, and looking at a large map on the wall. Above his workbench William Carey had nailed a map which showed all of the countries of the world. As he worked, his mind wandered to many far-off places. He thought of all the people in India who had never heard about Jesus.

His Bible, which he read often, told him that everyone should know about Jesus. But he didn't see any preachers going to India. So one day he said, "I'll go."

And he did go. Many thousands of miles across

the ocean to the land of India. He spent his life there. Working during the day, mending old shoes and making new pairs. Visiting people at night to tell them about Jesus. And after that, in the late hours, he worked writing a Bible that the Indian people could read in their own language.

Because of his life, there are thousands of Christians in India today. William Carey College in Calcutta was named after him. He was a missionary, a person who told others about Jesus.

One night William Carey took off his shoes (put empty shoes before children), went to bed, and died in his sleep. He left a pair of empty shoes. God fills these shoes with other missionaries. Maybe one of you. Who knows? You may some day be a missionary who goes to another country to tell others about Jesus.

Prayer: Dear Lord, thank You for all missionaries. If You want one of us to fill the empty shoes of William Carey, help us to hear and answer Your call. Amen.

31

WHAT DID YOU SAY?

Object: *A cassette tape recorder.*
Purpose: *To teach the proper and improper use of words.*

This is a tape recorder (*display*). And this is a tape (*remove cassette and display*). This little machine records voices on this tape, so that you can play back what you have heard.

Have you ever heard your voice on a tape recorder? Let's record your voices. After your voices have been recorded, we will listen. Each of you say, "God loves me." (*Record each voice individually.*)

Now let's listen to your voices. (*Let each child hear his voice.*)

The Bible tells us we need to be careful what we say. The words we speak. The way we talk to people. Words are very important.

Have you ever told a lie? Called someone a bad name? Said something that hurt somebody? Sometimes we say things that are bad.

Did you know that God hears every word we speak? That you and I have to answer for the things we say? I don't know if God has a tape recorder like this one that records everything I say, but I do know that He hears me speak and remembers everything I say.

Sometimes when God hears you speak, He says, "What did you say?" because He knows your words are not good.

So be careful when you speak. Say things that help, not hurt. Use your words to make people happy, not sad. That's the way God wants us to talk every day.

Prayer: Dear God, before I speak an unkind word, a cruel word, a hurting word, help me to remember that You are listening. Help me make You smile by the good words I say. Amen.

32

GOD IS COLORBLIND

Object: *A piece of red cellophane paper.*
Purpose: *To teach that God loves all people equally, regardless of their color of skin, and so should we.*

Have you ever taken a piece of cellophane like this candy wrapper, and looked through it? (*Place over eye.*) When I look at you through this red-colored paper, do you know what? You all look red! Everything looks red! This colored paper makes me see only one color—red!

Did you know that some persons cannot see certain colors? Their eyes do not see red or green or other colors. We call people who cannot see some colors *colorblind*. They are blind to certain colors.

Did you know that God is colorblind? He really is! Oh, not like people who can't see green or red. But when God looks at us He doesn't see what color our skin is. He doesn't see black people, or white people, or red people, or yellow people. He only sees *people*! People He loves. People He made. People He cares about very much.

And God says that we too should be colorblind like that. You and I should see people the way God sees people. We shouldn't think people are good or bad because they are yellow, or red, or black. We should see all people the way God sees them—as boys and girls and men and women whom God created just like Him. Did you know that? Every one of us is made like God.

And most of you are colorblind too. For children don't let a person's color of skin stand in their way.

But we adults sometimes do. And do you know what? We adults will try to make you see colors before you grow up. But don't let us. Always see people the way God does—as persons just like Him. That makes God very happy.

Prayer: God, we are so glad You made us, all of us, just like You. And You see us just as we are. Help us, Lord, to look on all people—black people, white people, yellow people, and red people—as people whom You love. Amen.

33

A SPECIAL MEAL

Object: *The elements of the Lord's Supper (or a bottle of grape juice and a loaf of bread).*
Purpose: *To make clear the meaning of the Lord's Supper.*

One day when Jesus was a boy his mother called him to eat. "Lunch time," she said. "Come in and eat your lunch. Your friends can eat with you."

Young Jesus and his friends ran to the home of Mary and Joseph to eat lunch together with Jesus' family. As everyone sat down at the table they saw a familiar sight. There on the table was a pitcher of rich red wine—a drink made from grapes that were crushed, very much like our grape juice. Also on the table was a large loaf of bread. It wasn't sliced. To get a piece you simply tore a piece off with your hand.

At every meal, Hebrew families like Jesus' sat down to drink wine and eat bread. They also had a special meal, called *Passover,* that helped them remember God's goodness.

Many years later, when Jesus was a man, He was eating a special meal with His friends. It was the day before Jesus was to die. And He knew it.

Jesus took the grape juice, turned to His friends and said, "This is my blood which is spilled for you." He took the bread and said, "This is my body which is broken for you—as often as you eat this bread and drink this juice you remember my death." Jesus wanted His friends to remember Him in this special way.

Today in our church we remember Jesus in this special way. By drinking this juice (*display*) and eating this bread (*display*) we remember that Jesus died for our sins.

When you are older and become a Christian, you too can eat this special meal that helps Christians remember Jesus' death on the cross for us.

Prayer: Thank You, God, for Jesus who died for our sins. Amen.

34

A GLASS OF WATER

Object: *A glass of water.*
Purpose: *To explain the meaning of Christian
baptism.*

Have you ever asked your mother, "May I have
a glass of water?" Sure you have, many times.
When you are thirsty, there is nothing that tastes
better than a glass of water (*display*).

When I was a little boy, I loved to visit my
grandfather's farm. One thing he let me do was to
get water from his well.

Did you know what a well is like? It's a deep
hole in the ground that has clean, pure water at the
bottom. I remember pulling up the rope. Up, up,
up (*dramatize*)—until finally a bucket full of water
came to the top.

Water is useful for so many things. Can you
name some of the ways we use water? (*Pause*.)

Yes, we drink it, we bathe in it, we wash clothes

in water, we cook food with it, we swim, fish, and ride boats in the water. Water is used in many ways.

Do you know the best way of all to use water? I think the happiest use of water is to baptize some-one.

Have you ever seen a baptism? Baptism is when a person asks the pastor to put them under water and raise them up again. That means something special. It means the person believes Jesus is the Son of God. Baptism is a way to say, "I believe Jesus died for my sins and came alive again." And that is the happiest of all ways to use water.

Prayer: Dear Father, how happy we are to see someone being baptized, going under water, and coming up to say, "I believe Jesus died for my sins and came alive again." Help us all to do that. Amen.

35

A REAL EASTER EGG

Object: *Empty egg shell (punctured at each end and with white and yolk blown out), which has been colored.*

Purpose: *To teach that Easter means Jesus is alive.*

There are many things that remind us of Easter—springtime, flowers, chocolate Easter bunnies in the store, Easter baskets, and Easter eggs. Have any of you been on an Easter egg hunt yet? Maybe you are going today! That's one of the fun things you do at Easter time—hunt Easter eggs.

Do you know how Easter eggs remind us of what Easter is all about? Let me tell you. When a mother hen or chicken sits on eggs, what happens? In a few weeks the eggs begin to crack and little baby chicks come out. An egg means new life. An egg reminds us there is new life inside that can come forth. That's what happened on Easter Sunday. Jesus came forth, with new life, out of the grave.

I call what I am holding a *real* Easter egg, and for a very special reason (*display*). If you break this egg open (*break egg shell*), it is empty. This is an empty Easter egg. And that is why I call this a real Easter egg. When Jesus died on the cross on Friday, He was then put in the grave, which was a cave where they bury dead people. Then they rolled a big stone in front of it, covering the door.

Do you know what happened on Sunday morning when they went to look inside that cave? Jesus wasn't there! Just like this Easter egg, the cave was empty. Why? Because Jesus had come alive.

He came alive because He was God. Jesus also said that anyone who believes in Him will never die—they will come alive too.

So I call this hollow Easter egg a *real Easter egg* because it's empty. It reminds me that when the women went to the cave and looked inside, Jesus wasn't there. He had come alive. And that is the real meaning of Easter, isn't it? Jesus Christ is alive! Because He lives, we live too. Let's pray and thank God for that.

Prayer: Father, I thank You for the empty cave on Easter Sunday. I'm glad that Jesus is alive, and that He gives me new life too. Amen.

36

A BUTTERFLY'S HOME

Object: *A cocoon.*
Purpose: *To teach the true meaning of Easter and
the reality of the resurrection of Jesus.*

Have you ever seen a caterpillar? They are little,
green worms—fuzzy crawlers that wiggle and
squirm on trees and on the ground.

Last October I was mowing my lawn, when,
right in the middle of my driveway, I saw it! A big,
fat, wiggly caterpillar. He was green and yellow.
He had fuzzy little hairs all over his body, and a big
horn on the front of his head.

I called my children to see this large caterpillar.
He must have been eating for days to be so fat! We
put him in a large jar, with some fresh leaves to eat.

Do you know what happened? One morning
when we went out to look at the caterpillar, he
wasn't there—at least we didn't think he was. But
in the jar we found something new—a cocoon!
(*Display*.) Here it is.

This cocoon is a house that the caterpillar lives
in during the winter. It protects him from the rain
and the cold. Any day now the cocoon is going to
open. And do you know what will come out of the

cocoon? (*Pause.*) No, not a caterpillar—a butterfly!

Every butterfly that you see fluttering in the air from flower to flower—the yellow ones, the black ones, the orange ones—all of them used to be caterpillars in a cocoon.

Today, Easter Sunday, is a special day. It reminds us that Jesus came alive out of the grave. After Jesus died on the cross, they put His body in a cave and rolled a stone in front of it. It was like the caterpillar wrapped in a cocoon. But the cave could not hold Him, just like the cocoon cannot hold the caterpillar. On the first Easter, Jesus came out of the cave alive, just like a butterfly will soon come out of this cocoon. And Jesus had a new body, just like the caterpillar gets a new body. Easter tells us that Jesus came alive, and we will come alive too, if we believe in Him.

Prayer: Father, thank You for Easter. How glad we are that Jesus came alive on Easter Sunday. And thank You, God, that we too have life eternal because we believe in Him. Amen.

37

WHAT IS A MOTHER?

Object: *A map, orange, thermometer, toy house, and the speaker's ear and ribs.*

Purpose: *To teach gratitude for the many ways a mother cares for her children.*

Today is Mother's Day. What is a mother? (*Allow answers.*) A mother is so many things. I have a few objects here that spell out the word *mother* and tell us something of what a mother is.

The first letter in the word *mother* is *m*. The name of this object (*unfold and display the map*) also begins with the letter *m*. This map reminds us that our mothers take us places—to school, to church, to a friend's house. A map reminds you that your mother spends a lot of time taking you places.

The second letter in *mother* is *o*. *O* is the first letter in *orange (display)*. An orange reminds us that mother fixes the food we eat and makes sure we eat the right food each day.

This thermometer (*display*) begins with *t*, the third letter in the word *mother*. When we are sick, our mother takes care of us and helps us get well. This thermometer reminds us of that.

H stands for *house* (*display toy house*). The fourth letter in the word *mother* helps us remember that she is the one who keeps our house clean and nice.

The next letter, *e,* stands for *ear* (*touch ear*). Whenever we call, she always hears us and helps us.

The last letter in the word *mother* is *r*. *R* is for *rib*. Do you know what a rib is? It's a bone right here (*touch a rib*), near our heart. Touch your rib. It's close to your heart and near to your side.

When God wanted to tell us how Eve, the first mother, was made, God said that He took a rib from her husband, Adam, and created the first mother.

Aren't you glad that God gave you a mother? She helps you in so many ways. And most of all, your mother loves you. Let's thank God for our mothers.

Prayer: Dear God, thank You for our mothers who love us and care for us in so many ways. Amen.

38

FIRECRACKERS AND FAITH

Object: *A firecracker.*
Purpose: *To teach that the story of Jesus is powerful.*

Next Wednesday is July four. That's a special
day. What happens on the Fourth of July? (*Pause.*)
When I was a little boy, I remember waking up on
the Fourth of July to the sound of pow-pow-pow.
Firecrackers! (*Display.*) One thing we do on the
Fourth of July is pop firecrackers. It is a way of
celebrating our country's birthday. America was
born on the Fourth of July. That is what we cele-
brate.

Did you know that the Bible says the story of
Jesus is like a firecracker? The Bible tells us the
story of Jesus is like dynamite. Now a stick of
dynamite is actually a very big firecracker. It's
very powerful. So the Bible tells us this story of
Jesus is really explosive.

Just like this firecracker, the story of Jesus has

great power. It has the power to change a nation. The people who first came to America wanted a land where they could worship God. Our country was founded to allow everyone to worship God without fear. Our laws and our government were written by men who believed the story of Jesus. That is one reason why America has been a power-ful nation—the story of Jesus has made us great.

The story of Jesus can also make *you* great. It is powerful enough to change your life and make you strong.

So as you come to church and learn about Jesus, listen very closely. For the story of Jesus is just like this firecracker. It is powerful. It can change you and make you great.

Prayer: Dear God, You are so strong and we are so weak. Let the power of Jesus explode in us that we may be changed into better persons. Amen.

39

GOD AND GOBLINS

Object: *A Halloween mask or pumpkin.*
Purpose: *To teach the reality of God.*

(*Display mask or pumpkin.*) Next week is Halloween! A happy day for children. Every boy and girl likes to dress up as a witch, a ghost, or a goblin and go trick or treating. Halloween is fun!

But do you know how Halloween got started? Long ago, November 1 was called *All Saints Day*. It was thought to be a very special day honoring the great saints—people who loved God and did remarkable things for God.

Because it was such a holy day, the people believed that the night just before All Saints Day was a night of evil. People believed that all the bad spirits roamed around on the evening before this hallowed (or holy) day. This *Halloween* as it was called, was the evening just before All Saints Day when ghosts and goblins did evil things.

Now I don't believe in goblins or ghosts. I don't believe evil spirits do bad things on Halloween. It's all make-believe, something we dream up in our minds for fun and games.

Sometimes, however, we think God is like the goblins. Just a storybook character someone created. Not a real person. Just a make-believe person.

Let me tell you, God is not like a goblin. He is *real*. He is *alive*. God made you and me. He hears us when we pray. He takes care of us every day.

Yes, God is real. He is with us *every* day, not just on holy days. I'm glad God is real and is near us all the time. Aren't you?

Prayer: Dear God, thank You for being here with us right now. And thank You for being at our side all the time. Amen.

40

FIVE KERNELS OF CORN

Object: *Five kernels of corn.*
Purpose: *To teach each child to be grateful to God.*

Last week I was visiting a school. In the hall I saw many posters. They were all pictures about Thanksgiving. One said:

"We Have Thanksgiving
Because We Are Thankful For:
1. Our Schools
2. Our Homes
3. Our Families
4. Our Churches
5. Our Food
6. Our Country

But the poster did not mention *who* we are to thank. To be thankful, you have to thank somebody. You can't be thankful *for* things unless you are thankful *to* someone.

The first Thanksgiving was a time when the Pilgrims thanked someone. Now they did not have much to be thankful for. The Pilgrims faced hard times after coming to the New World. There were periods of starvation in the colony both before and after the first Thanksgiving service. For a time food was so scarce that the daily ration was only five kernels of corn per person (*display*).

Can you imagine that? What if you sat down to eat your dinner and your mother brought you only five kernels of corn? That wouldn't be much to eat!

The Pilgrims did not have much to eat the first Thanksgiving. Later, when crops were good, the Pilgrims established the custom of placing beside their plates five kernels of corn as a memorial of those difficult days. It was a way to thank God for His blessings.

That simple custom is nice. Next Thursday as we sit down to our bountiful tables for our Thanksgiving meal, let's place beside our plate five kernels of corn. What better way can we remember God's blessing and our abundance?

Before we can be thankful *for something*, we must be thankful *to someone*. Let's all thank God for His goodness.

Prayer: Dear Lord, at this Thanksgiving season we remember Your goodness and thank You, God, for everything. Amen.